Etiquette
for
SNOBS

SOCIALLY NECESSARY OCCASIONS AND BUSINESS SITUATIONS

by Michele Goodman-Jones

Etiquette for SNOBS: Socially Necessary Occasions and Business Situations

Books may be purchased for book club, educational, business, and promotional use. For information, email **trymern@aol.com** with your request.

ISBN **9798607938420**

FIRST EDITION

Printed in the United States of America

Book Design by Stephen V. Ramey

Cover background design by www.123Freevectors.com

Dedicated to my mother and father

Dolores and Lewis Goodman

and my siblings

Clarence, Janet, and Leslie

INTRODUCTION

Etiquette is a French word that means label, ticket, or card. The word sometimes makes people uncomfortable and self-conscious. The first thing people assume when I mention etiquette is table manners, but there is so much more. Every aspect of our lives has guidelines about appropriate behavior in different situations.

Understanding the importance of etiquette gives you the "ticket" you need to be comfortable and able to handle the myriad of situations you encounter. It puts you at ease and everyone around you.

The history of etiquette goes back to the beginning of mankind. There are lots of passages in the Bible that are instructional about how people should treat one another. How a husband should treat his wife and how a mother handles her children. The bible speaks to proper dress and that children should honor their parents.

The Middle Ages gave us examples of strict behavior and unusual social skills. During this period we started to cover our mouths when we yawned and could no longer put our elbows on the table because we sat so close together there was no room for elbows. Superstition influenced the development of many etiquette rules although often they were just matters of logic.

The late 1800's started modern etiquette or American etiquette because we had millionaires who were looking for ways for separate themselves from the common person. Men started to bow, and little girls curtsied, men did not smoke in the presence of a woman and women did not smoke at all. Newspapers reported what the wealthy New York families known as The Four

Hundreds, were doing and etiquette columns told them how to do it correctly.

After two World Wars, the Great Depression, the Fabulous 40's and the Fit-in 50's etiquette still ruled as important, but that changed during the 60's and 70's. Disobedience ushered in an era of rebellion with hippies, the drug culture, long hair, black power, women's liberation, denim, etc. This started the decline in manners.

But the decades since the 70's have brought about a tremendous change. Global shrinkage from the electronic revolution has connected people from different cultures and backgrounds like never before.

Etiquette is learned! No one is born with etiquette genes and this book is written to give you an idea of what to do with the everyday SITUATIONS you will face. You may have better solutions to effectively deal with these SITUATIONS but this book is designed to give you another viewpoint.

Enjoy and have fun reading about SNOBS.

Situations

Professional

Magic Words 3
Big Thank You 4
Drop Calls 5
Handshake 6
Shaking Hands Behind Desk 7
The Business Card 8
Professional Personnel 9
Coworkers 10
Dress Down Friday 11
Is It a Compliment? 12
Compliments (Part 1) 13
Compliments (Part 2) 14

Let the Party Begin

Washing Your Hands 19
The Napkin 20
Large Portions 21
Salt and Pepper — The Couple 22
Who Pays for the Meal 23
Take Home Food 24
Tipping 25
Clumsy at the Table 26
Bring Something 27
Champagne 28
Style of Eating 29
Chopsticks 31
Sharing Potato Chips/Double Dipping 32

Not Sure What to Do

How to Get Rid of Guests 37

When to Leave a Friend's House 38

When to Leave Events 39

Partying Neighbors 40

Gift Giving 41

Theme Events 42

Posting Pictures 43

And More

Your Car Trunk 47

Money for Gasoline 48

Lipstick on the Teeth 49

Changed Your Deodorant 50

Table Cough 51

Kiss Kiss Cheek to Cheek 52

Shopping 53

The Ugly American 54

I Need to Pee 55

Handling Money 56

Pet Etiquette 57

You Look Tired 59

Weight Gain 60

Teachable Moments With Kids 61

Professional Situations

Magic Words

I am currently in a contract with a local school district and my course is about character building and manners. These young minds are open and ready to be stimulated with fresh new ideas. My intro into all my training with young people is to introduce the Magic Words.

Magic Words have become obsolete to most people and I am counting on the young folks to revive these words. I think if more adults started to use the Magic Words again, we could eliminate some of the hostility that exists and we would have a kinder calmer world.

PLEASE, THANK YOU, FORGIVE ME, I'M SORRY, NO THANKS, I LOVE YOU. Some people refuse to say these simple, powerful words. These are the words that a SNOB would say because a SNOB knows the power that they carry. SNOBS know that to be kind, considerate, and well respected you have to say "PLEASE" sometimes.

BIG THANK YOU

This etiquette rule is simple. The bigger the gift the bigger the thank you. An example would be: You receive a car, baby grand piano, trip to Rome, a large check, or anything over the top. You always say "thank you" upon receiving the gift but you must do more. Jump up and down, clap your hands, run in a circle, you get the picture, but that's not all you do. You must remember to send a thank you note and periodically say thank you again, and again, until they are tired of hearing it.

I loaned money to a friend and when she paid it back she sent flowers to my job with a note and when I got home there was another bouquet of my favorite flowers. It was a double thank you.

Remember, the bigger the gift the bigger the thank you.

DROP CALLS

You're on the phone and you get disconnected. Who calls back? The person who made the initial call is the one who calls back. This will alleviate the back and forth calling, trying to reach the other person. If you're having problems with your telephone let the other person know that you will call them back if you get disconnected.

HANDSHAKE

Most people that I encounter do not shake hands correctly. It's a very simple thing to do but for some reason it's not done properly. Women for the most part shake hands too softly, as if they are supposed to show their femininity in the connection. Handshaking is not hard or soft, but firm. Make eye contact, 2 or 3 pumps. The web of the hands should be touching and that is the key to keeping someone from crushing your hand. The web prevents you from squeezing too hard and that is the secret to a successful handshake.

Remember to stand when you are shaking hands, if you can. It's very disrespectful to remain seated while shaking hands, especially to an older person. This applies to men and women.

SHAKING HANDS BEHIND DESK

If you happen to be behind a desk and you need to shake hands with someone, stand up and come from behind the desk if possible. You should always stand up whenever you are shaking hands if the situation permits. Both men and women should stand.

THE BUSINESS CARD

Business card etiquette is an area where SNOBS fall short. When handed a business card, flier, etc., please take a look at the card that is handed to you. It only takes 5 seconds to acknowledge the "gift" that you have just received. If you have time make a comment about the card. "You work on Wall Street" or "I like the design of your card."

Many people will take a card and automatically put it away without a glance. The person who gave you the card is insulted and the hours they put in creating this"gift" are not noticed. People value their cards and want you to LOOK at it, if only for a second. You may not want the card but be well mannered.

It is not polite to shove a card on someone, you should wait until you are asked for the card. The exception would be a meet-and-greet where sharing information is expected.

Later when you have time make your notes on the back of the card, i.e., date, place, event, and anything pertinent. Three months later you will be glad you did. A SNOB will use this information to come across as sharp whenever you need to talk to or meet that person again.

PROFESSIONAL PERSONNEL

Like most people there are times when you have an appointment at a business office, doctor's office, court, banks, etc. I have noticed that the personnel in many of these establishments treat you like you should know what they know. They are there to provide you with information and they reluctantly give you the information you need with an attitude or make you feel stupid for asking questions.

Recently I encountered a miserable woman sitting at one of those sign-in windows you see in doctors' offices and elsewhere. I stood at the window and, for about 30 seconds, I did not know I was supposed to sign in. I finally asked if I should sign in and she replies "yes" in a condescending tone as if I were stupid. This was my first time in the office. She never said "good morning" or "may I help you." In fact she never looked up to see me.

People who work with the public need to practice common courtesies and use the Magic Words if only to make an uncomfortable encounter easier. People who are nervous in a new situation may need your direction. Never assume they know what you get paid to know. The public keeps you employed so treat them with respect.

COWORKERS

It's always better if you get along with your coworkers. You may not really like the people you work with, but being polite pays off. You don't want to be left out of the loop about things that are happening around you at work. Periodically go to lunch with the group if you're invited. Donate to the different office occasions, i.e., baby shower, wedding, funeral, or retirement, if your funds permit.

Being cordial is important if you want promotions or plan to be there for the long haul. I personally know that being nice to everyone you work with makes life so much easier.

DRESS DOWN FRIDAY

In the 70's and 80's my generation dressed up on Friday to go out after work for Happy Hour, especially the Yuppies (Young Urban Professionals) and Buppies (Black Urban Professionals). Restaurants & bars would offer lots of free hors d'oeuvre with the half price drinks and everyone looked so successful. Men and women wore suits with all the right accessories, so the hot spots in the city looked like Wall Street.

Today we dress down most of the time, even professional corporations have banished the suit. Some companies have casual Friday and people love this casual look. My sister refused to relax her way of dressing when the trend started in the 90's; she kept the professional look while people around her started dressing badly, which made her stand out more. She will tell you that a lot of her success with the bank for which she worked was because she always looked and acted like a professional no matter what the trend.

If you're serious about your life, keep the focus. If you look like a joke, don't get upset if you're treated that way. Pull yourself together and look your best, life will be easier and doors will open up for you. That you can take to the bank!

Is It a Compliment?

When giving someone words of encouragement watch the words you select. An example "You're not a <u>bad</u> tennis player." Why not just say, "You're a good tennis player." Using the word <u>bad</u> can take some of the specialness out of the compliment. Another example: "You're not <u>bad</u> looking." It's better to say, "You're good looking."

COMPLIMENTS (PART 1)

Someone is nice enough to give you a compliment about the unique pair of shoes you are wearing and you reply, "These old shoes, I've had these for years." You have just made the person feel stupid, by making them come across like they have no fashion sense. Never make a person feel stupid by giving you kind words.

COMPLIMENTS (PART 2)

As a young woman in the beauty industry you are always aware of your appearance, as well as everyone around you. That is the nature of the beauty business. Quite often I would get a compliment about my appearance and many times it was positive. Someone would say to me "You're so pretty for a black woman/ darker skinned woman/African American woman, etc. and I would reply with a puzzled look on my face and they would repeat the statement again as if I didn't hear it the first time. This statement always makes me confused, would I not be pretty if I was lighter, or was it hard to believe that anything dark could be so beautiful? If they had just said you're "pretty" I could understand that I was just given a compliment.

Let the Party Begin

Situations

WASHING YOUR HANDS

Whenever you touch door knobs, banisters, menus, railings, etc., you are touching other peoples' germs. Shaking hands, touching pets and kids, more germs. I see people playing with their hair while cooking in the kitchen without washing their hands. Then we walk into a restaurant or a friend's house and start to eat with our dirty hands. Sometimes we put our dirty hands into a bag of chips and the contamination goes on. The car steering wheel is unclean so it's wise to have towelettes in the car for drive thru meals.

As a child, my mother always told us to wash our hands before we helped prepare food and before we sat at the dinner table. Sometimes when I wash my hands I'm surprised that the water is dirty because my hands look and feel clean. Washing your hands makes other people comfortable and that's worth it.

THE NAPKIN

Please don't wrap the dinner napkin around your neck in public while dining. You will come across as a big baby with a bib. This will give you a lower rating and make you look gauche. When I see this action across the restaurant I want to send you a note on "Table Manners in Public." The napkin around the neck never looks good in public. Even if your daddy does it, it's country.

Ladies should carry a scarf that can be placed around the neck for a temporary bib to catch spills, especially at an all white attire event. Nothing ruins a pretty silhouette like a strange spot on a fabulous outfit. You can remove the scarf after it is no longer needed.

If you are in the comfort of your home, do whatever makes you feel at home. I tend to enjoy practicing good etiquette behavior, so it's a part of my normal flow, it now feels comfortable being formal.

LARGE PORTIONS

Many times at an outing I've noticed a situation that is quite disturbing. You see a long line of people waiting to get food and you see the people at the beginning of the line with double servings of food (especially meat) on their plates. Unfortunately the people at the end of the line will get whatever is left.

I've noticed at cocktail receptions that people pile high the hors d'oeuvre on the first go round and this makes you look pathetic. The plates are small for a reason. You can always go back.

It is really embarrassing to see a person pile a plate at a buffet, because you can always go back for more. This is very important, if it's a small event or a house gathering where the food may be limited.

The Etiquette Rule is: Start with a single portion of food and after everyone has a plate of food it's okay to go back for a second helping.

SALT AND PEPPER — THE COUPLE

Some years ago I had one of those learning experiences that come to you unexpectedly. I was dining with some people I didn't know and I casually asked for the pepper. Salt is something I never use at the table and I was handed the salt and pepper shakers. I took them both and wondered why I was given both. That was not the first time this has happened to me so it made me question myself. Years later as I developed my Etiquette training I learned that salt and pepper are like a married couple, they dance around the table together. Don't try to divorce them, they are a couple.

WHO PAYS FOR THE MEAL

At the end of the meal in a restaurant someone asks to help you pay the bill and you say "No, I got this," don't go back and forth about who pays. If someone insists on paying the bill, let them. It may be that they feel better if they handle the transaction. You can always suggest that you leave the tip (in cash). The etiquette rule is: "Whoever makes the offer for dinner should pay."

Take Home Food

People in New Castle, PA cook lots of extra food so that guests can take something home. This concept is new for me because the etiquette rule is "If you come empty handed, you leave empty handed." That rule does not apply in this town. People who come to eat will wrap a plate to go before they sit down to eat. The first time I encountered this strange custom, I didn't understand why people would wrap up food for people not in attendance or for their lunch the next day. It made no sense to me.

The cook would have to double all the portions to be able to feed all of these extra people and that is costly. What about having leftovers for your family the following day, will anything be left? Now I see it as special, a way of sharing with family and friends.

Enjoy the food while you are visiting and only take something home if it is offered to you. Dessert is always okay to wrap and take home.

TIPPING

Years ago tipping was done before the meal. Tipping means **To Insure Promptness** and by giving a tip beforehand you insure that your service will be better. Today, **TIPS** means **To Insure Proper Service.**

Never pull out a calculator if the meal is under $100. There are several ways to figure out a tip that are very simple. One thing you can do is double the tax and round up to the next dollar. If you leave a $1 bill for every $5 you spend that is 20% of the bill. A SNOB will leave a 20% tip and that is a good tip. If you're cheap at least $1 from everyone seated at the table. A minimum tip is $1.

My sister is a server at an upscale restaurant and says she prefers they have the tip in cash if possible. Don't punish servers by not leaving a tip for things that they cannot control, and leaving a bunch of pennies is childish and something a SNOB would never do.

CLUMSY AT THE TABLE

I have been clumsy since I was a child and today I have been known to knock over a thing or two at the table, especially something tall like candlesticks, water, bowls, and flowers. If this unfortunate situation happens to you remember to downplay the situation. Keep conversation flowing while trying to clean the mess and flag a server. Play it down. The important thing is to not make a big deal of the situation. If the incident happens to someone with you, give them some help and continue the conversation.

BRING SOMETHING

Are you the person who never brings anything to the party or your friend's house? Hopefully you don't eat or drink a lot when someone invites you over. It's not that you need to bring something each and every time you come, but one out of three visits should include a treat of some kind. Wine, chips, beer, pizza, soda, etc. Make a contribution to the gathering and stay in good standing.

CHAMPAGNE

My all-time favorite treat is a cold glass of champagne. I was introduced to champagne in 1983 with my friend and business partner, Toi. We had just opened our store "Try Me Boutique" and someone gave us several bottles of champagne at the grand opening and that was the wakeup call for our tastebuds. We started serving champagne to our customers on Saturdays.

Champagne is an acquired taste and most people don't enjoy the favor initially. It still makes a nice gift because you can make mimosas by adding orange juice or pass it forward to someone who enjoys the sparkling wine. Having a bottle handy is a nice festive surprise and people feel special whenever they are served a glass.

STYLE OF EATING

I f you are a true SNOB you have to be able to eat in all types of situations. I remember being told at the young age of 23 that I needed lots of training if I wanted to really be sophisticated. I thought I was sophisticated. That's before I understood the difference between Class and Sophistication.

The older woman was going to teach me a thing or two about the different styles of eating. I reluctantly listened to this woman who explained "American Style" vs. "European Style" or "Continental Style." I felt this was not something I would need, but the SNOB in me was curious so I went home and started to practice this useless skill. Ten years letter I went on a second interview with Revlon North America at the Detroit International Airport. It happened to be in one of those private clubs. It was my first time in one of these SNOB airport clubs and it was a wakeup call, I didn't know they existed. Nice places to hang out if you're waiting for a plane.

My future boss was sitting with his boss and they had gotten started eating because they had a flight back to New York. They were both eating "Continental Style" and I ate my food the same style as these two men. My boss later told me my "sophisticated" table manners were impressive as the job called for a lot of social interactions, he was comfortable with me after seeing my table manners at that meal.

I learned two things about business that day. One, be

prepared. It was 10 years of practicing before my flexible style of eating made a difference. Two, sometimes your manners will give you the edge you need when you least expect it. His boss must have been impressed too.

CHOPSTICKS

I started practicing the art of chopsticks in my twenties. The woman who informed me that I was not sophisticated also included chopsticks in my unofficial training. I did inform her that whenever I go to a Chinese restaurant there's always silverware, so why did I need to learn another useless skill. Once again the SNOB in me loved the challenge and the dexterity of this new skill and I began to practice with popcorn. Of course it was in the privacy of my home because I did not want anyone to see me fumble with these two sticks.

During the 1980's I was asked to go on a date and fly to New York City. This was when People Airline had trips to NYC for $29.00. My date wanted to take me to the best Chinese restaurant in Chinatown. No one in the restaurant was using silverware and because I had practiced for years I was able to come out of the closet and show off my skill. My date assumed that any real SNOB would know how to use these utensils. I would have been embarrassed if I had had to ask for a fork. He obviously assumed I used chopsticks.

I find that when I am dining in an Asian restaurant using chopsticks is always a nice SNOBBY thing to do because most Americans use forks. This is worth learning and it's fun.

SHARING POTATO CHIPS/DOUBLE DIPPING

If you have not washed your hands you should not place them in a bag of chips being shared by others. Take a napkin and use it like a glove to reach inside the bag. You can also shake some chips onto a napkin. This snob technique goes for popcorn, pretzels, etc.

Please don't be the double dipper at the party. If you didn't get enough dip on that chip get a spoon and put some extra dip on a separate plate and dip away.

I get asked whether you should use the dip again after the dipper has been there. That's a personal choice, but the host should remove the dip if someone is caught double dipping. Nothing needs to be said, no one needs to be embarrassed. The host simply removes the dip carefully to replace it promptly with unsullied dip.

Not Sure What to Do

Situations

How to Get Rid of Guests

As soon as a guest arrives, set the stage from the beginning. This is important if your time is limited. Tell them up front that you have two hours before you need to get ready. Somewhere in the next hour mention once again that you have something to do and in a few minutes you will need to take a shower or get dressed. Ask them what the rest of their day is like. You have to start having the goodbye conversation with the guest as you start putting things away.

WHEN TO LEAVE A FRIEND'S HOUSE

Everyone I know has complained about the person who stays too long. They come to visit, get very relaxed and four hours later they are still in your home. If you have kids and/or a husband they should have been gone, a couple of hours is enough. An exception would be that you are working on a project or having an event at your home. If you are being offered another meal it's time to go.

Single people or lonely people may not care, but you should be cognizant of other peoples' time. A SNOB will sense that it's time to go.

When to Leave Events

There is no one answer to fit all situations but it's safe to say the one hour rule works for most unimportant situations. Weddings, receptions, showers, commencements, and political events you want to stay until the pinnacle of the event has occurred. If it's a shower stay until the gifts are opened. If it's a political gathering stay until the main speech is finished. If you can't stay for the pinnacle just stay one hour and you will be a SNOB in good standing.

PARTYING NEIGHBORS

Loud neighbors can be a nightmare but there are ways to handle this dilemma. If you are having a noisy event (music, bands, deejay, dancers) invite any neighbors who would be affected by the noise. They probably will not come, but extend the invitation. It's a good idea to turn the volume down around 10:00 pm.

Gift Giving

Giving or receiving a gift is always a special occasion and everyone has a special role. Whenever possible open your gift in the presence of the person who has given it to you. The giver wants to see your expression, watch your body language, and hear the excitement in your voice. Sometimes as you shop for a gift you can imagine the other person's surprise or excitement and that's the fun for you, the gift giver.

By all means, try not to rip beautiful expensive paper off the gift as if it is meaningless, The paper is part of the gift so remove it carefully. It's a ritual to be shared by all involved. The bows, ribbon, paper, etc. are all a part of the artwork of putting a gift together and all these items have a cost. You should acknowledge the workmanship and fuss over the exterior before you see what's inside.

If you don't like the gift, be a SNOB and show your gratitude and say, "Thank You." Never complain. Just be a class act and smile.

THEME EVENTS

Over the past decade people have been giving a lot of theme parties. The "All White Party" where all of the guests wear white is a popular theme. If you are going to a theme party, you should try to follow the theme if possible, unless it is optional. If it's not optional and you want to do your own thing, or you don't have the clothing, it's best you don't go. If the event is labeled formal, informal, black tie, etc., get more information, don't guess.

People plan theme parties for a reason, otherwise it would not be a theme party. Don't mess up the fantasy someone may have envisioned for their event. Stay home if you don't like the theme.

You can always call and explain your dilemma. They may be happy just to have you at the event.

POSTING PICTURES

Technology has made it easy to take pictures of our lives. We see photos of friends and family everywhere and it is amazing. Without Facebook, Instagram, Google, etc., I would not be as informed. Occasionally we have to stop and remember to stay positive with these options. Remember that people should be asked if they are okay with having their picture on social media. Not everyone is okay with this freedom we take with our cameras.

I had a friend who started taking pictures in my house and she never asked permission. My house is not public and I may not want the whole wide world to look inside my house at any time for the unlimited future. I told her I was not okay with her taking the pictures and she removed the pictures to make me comfortable. If I want to take pictures and show them off that's my prerogative. Many people may not be so accommodating. Another reason why etiquette training is so important.

In private settings you should ask permission and make sure everyone's okay with you posting their picture, especially people you don't know. Private citizens may be offended.

And More

Situations

Your Car Trunk

Besides the obvious safety items you have in your trunk it's always a smart idea to include some practical things. In a small box you can have an extra pair of comfortable shoes, blanket, shawl, tissues, paper towels, aspirin, umbrella, binoculars, contact lens kit, bottle of wine in a gift bag, etc. In the summer I keep a folding chair in the trunk and a small generic gift for emergencies.

I see empty trunks that are so clean, as if a prize is going to be awarded for not having anything in the trunk. What is the purpose of not being prepared, you have the space. People with such trunks can't give you a tissue if you sneeze. SNOBS stay prepared.

My friends remark that I have too many things in my car, but every time they need something (sunglasses, etc.) that I can provide, they are grateful.

MONEY FOR GASOLINE

Often we want to give someone money for gas and they won't take it. First of all, anyone who drives a car needs gas to keep it going, so don't ask if they need gas, they might have a full tank, but tanks don't stay full.

If the person is uncomfortable taking the gas money from you just leave it on the seat, glove box, or ash tray and get out the car. I promise you they will not run you down to give it back.

Drivers appreciate the money for gas and if you are always riding with someone, even if they are not going out of their way to transport you, do your part. SNOBS know better.

LIPSTICK ON THE TEETH

Last Christmas I had a lovely event in the lobby of the building I manage and lots of pictures were being taken. My neighbor took a nice picture of Perry and me and I noticed my teeth were covered with red lipstick. My lipstick was covering my teeth and it looked like blood. I can't believe no one mentioned this to me. I was the emcee for the night and all I can think about is my red mouth talking to the crowd. Please let someone know they have a situation going on and they will be grateful, not embarrassed.

Changed Your Deodorant

There comes a time when you need to tell someone something that may not be easy.

It could be about an odor, gossip, appearance, whatever. Whether or not the person is sensitive is not the point, the advice is the same. Always say something positive before you say something that may be hurtful. "You always smell so nice, but I notice lately you've changed your deodorant." Telling someone in a kind way gets the point across, softens the blow, and saves friendships. If you follow this good before bad formula, it will make all your uncomfortable situations a little brighter.

TABLE COUGH

Suddenly you have to sneeze or cough and you don't have time to get a handkerchief so you reach for the next best thing, the napkin. Take the napkin off your lap and put it completely over your mouth, turn your head away and sneeze. Turn back to the table and say "excuse me" and that's all. Don't explain that you have been under the weather or describe your allergies. Just continue the conversation like nothing happened. You always downplay situations at the table.

Kiss Kiss Cheek to Cheek

Air kissing can cause a collision if you don't know the correct way to air kiss. You always put right cheek against right cheek, then left check to left cheek. If you follow these instructions you will not have a head on collision.

SHOPPING

The next time you go food shopping and someone has a few items and you have a full shopping cart of food, let them go in front of you. By the time you organize your food on the conveyer belt they will be finished and out the door. So you really have not lost any time.

This common courtesy is appreciated by everyone who has one or two items.

THE UGLY AMERICAN

When you travel to other countries and the first language of that country is not English learn the Magic Words and a few phrases. Please, thank you, good morning, you get the picture. The first question you should learn to say is "Do you speak English?" That's just being polite and respectful. Outside of the United States most countries have English as a second language and they will be able to communicate with you but it's very disrespectful to not be able to say *something* to them in their language, in their country. Be a SNOB and learn a few cool things to say.

On a trip to Italy in 2004, I put on my headset, listened to a tape in the airplane and by the time I arrived in Rome, I had a few Italian phrases I was able to say. It made the trip more enjoyable being able to practice with the Italians.

I Need to Pee

This public announcement is absolutely disgusting. If you need to go to the restroom and you tell everyone that you have to "pee" that personal information does not need to be shared with anyone. Children may say "pee" but not an adult. A SNOB would know better.

In my early 20's I remember saying "I have to pee" on a first date. My date expressed his disappointment in my choice of words and that was the first and last date. A true lady would never let the word come out of her mouth, especially in mixed company.

HANDLING MONEY

It's always best to give someone payment in an envelope whether it's cash or check, especially if you are paying people in public. My housekeeper receives her money in an envelope whenever she's finished and it makes the transaction more professional. If you owe someone money give it back to them in an envelope and include a note, or you can write "thank you" on the outside of the envelope. Little gestures like this make you a class act and a true SNOB.

PET ETIQUETTE

I am a pet owner and I love my dog and cat. I didn't grow up with pets, so my love for these animals came later in life. I started liking cats when I got my first apartment. I was cleaning my new apartment before the move and discovered an empty box of D-Con in the back of a cabinet. I have alway been scared of mice so I realized I might have a visitor. I went to the Humane Society in Pittsburgh and purchased my first cat. After a few months I became a cat lover. When I married my husband Perry, he came with a dog and now I am a lover of dogs.

I had to learn pet etiquette, it was a learning experience and adjustment. Cultural differences dictate what direction you should go. My friends look at pets (almost) like family. They will not allow the cat to walk across the dinner table or sit on the kitchen counter. The big dog will not be sleeping in the bed with the family, he will have his own bed. Some people allow the dogs/cats to roam freely among guests and others put the dog/cat away during large gatherings.

Some people do not want your animal in their house, no matter how lovable. Most people want their pet to be comfortable at home and you must decide if you want to be there. Don't complain about someone's pet in their house. You leave if you are uncomfortable. You also have the right to deny their pet entry. If you are in doubt ask before you come with little Charlie.

If you handle your pet often make sure your guests

see you wash your hands from time to time. Some things you do for the comfort of other people.

You Look Tired

As we age, especially women, we can sometimes appear to look a little worn. The aging process can start to show on the face and with aging comes sagging. You can be wrinkle free, but gravity has taken root.

When you say "You look tired" to an older woman it's like saying "You look older." No woman wants to hear that she looks bad, especially after she has worked out, eaten a healthy breakfast, dressed to impress and is feeling fabulous. She may not be tired at all and then suddenly she's told she looks tired.

Some people can afford to have corrective surgery and make improvements to the way they look. For everyone else we have to accept our DNA and do the best we can.

In the cosmetic industry you never want a person to feel bad so you select words that make people feel good. If you run into someone you haven't seen in a long time and they look "tired" say something kind and not mention the way they look. We should always say something positive and leave the encounter feeling uplifted.

WEIGHT GAIN

I started my first weight gain in my forties and the next weight gain in menopause. During my thin years I could eat anything and not gain an ounce. Back in the 70's I used a product called "Weigh On" for weight gain and I went to an Elaine Powers Salon to exercise to build bulk. I wanted to be heavier and not have bony legs, knees, arms, and shoulders. People made comments and told me I was too thin.

I am sensitive about making comments to a person about his or her weight gain or weight loss. Unless you know the reason for the change, it's best not to say anything. Even skinny people get annoyed if their weight is always a topic of conversation. People too tall or too short don't need to be reminded about their uniqueness over and over again. They know what they look like.

People who haven't seen me in years expect me to look thinner, like I did when I modeled in the 70's and 80's. Today I'm enjoying my fluffy silhouette. Those critics have also experienced a bit of fluffiness over the years. Fortunately, my career was not based on my size, but other talents God gave me.

Once again say something pleasant, "Good to see you. You look happy."

TEACHABLE MOMENTS WITH KIDS

Since I have never been a parent I have to be careful about judging people who are. I want to state that I admire what you do and you have my blessing, because it really looks hard.

Looking at the situation from the outside I see the skill, love, and patience that it takes to raise a child and I also see the things that are so damaging, disappointing, and unforgivable.

One thing that I have noticed over the years when I am watching adults with children is yelling at kids in public. Kids will do things they shouldn't and they need to be disciplined, but it should be a learning experience. If the adult tells the kid to stop and does not give an explanation, I wonder if the kid has learned anything at all. I heard a mother tell her son that if he kept playing with something hot, he would get burned and be put in the hospital and away from the family. The kid looked like he was understanding the consequences. That was a teachable moment. If the mother had only said "stop" that was really not enough information to make an impact.

As a non-mother who works with kids I try to create as many teachable moments as I can.

About the Author

For more than 30 years Michele has been passionate about teaching manners, etiquette, and grooming to the public at large. Since the 90's she has shared her knowledge to groups and individuals around the country. The nickname "The Empress of Etiquette" is the perfect title for this hard working consultant.

Michele began her career in the beauty and fashion business working for the largest cosmetic and retail companies in the world. Model, makeup artist, cosmetic/fragrance buyer, boutique owner, and speaker, but being a wife is the greatest gift of all.

Special thanks

Special thanks to my husband Perry for making this book a reality. Without you this would not have been possible.

I want to give a big thank you to Garrett Whitehouse for his technical skills that put it all together.

Dr. Validia Giddens' kind words and keen insight helped me to get the title right. Thanks for not being selfish with your incredible mind.

Last but not least, my aunt Gladys Goodman who started this etiquette journey in the 80's with her Etiquette Tea parties that opened my eyes to a rewarding business.